C000225090

Will Young

On Camera: Off Duty

Text by Richard Galpin

Polaroids by Faye Anthony

© 19 Merchandising Ltd 2003
Management: Simon Fuller at 19 Management Ltd

This edition published in 2004 by
Virgin Books
Thames Wharf Studios
Rainville Road
London W6 9HA

First published by Contender Books 2003.

The moral right of Richard Galpin to be identified as the author of this work has been asserted by him in accordance with the Copyright, Designs and Patents Act, 1988.

All rights reserved.

ISBN 1 85227 199 X

Polaroids by Faye Anthony
Concert photographs by Jeff Spicer

Design by designsection, Frome, Somerset
Repro by Radstock Repro, Midsomer Norton, Bath
Printed and bound in Great Britain by Butler & Tanner Ltd, Frome and London
Production by Kate Gribble

On Camera: Off Duty

Contents

Introduction

To begin with, I feel it is important to explain my thinking behind this third book. When I started out I had very specific ideas on making a book that was perhaps slightly different from the norm while allowing you guys a more intimate and fun look at moments which are never really seen on the TV – and there are some funny (hopefully!) captions on the polaroids which I have put on to let you know what I was doing. I hope it shows two things in particular: firstly how much I enjoy the fashion side of things and what a wonderful team of people I work with on that front, and secondly how much fun we have when we're working. I remember when someone asked me after winning the show – 'When do you think you would ever stop?', I replied 'When singing stops being enjoyable' – and I think you can tell that I'm still enjoying it!

I also have to thank the people who have made this book possible and fun at the same time! Thank you to Maya for her broad-thinking and patience, to Charlotte for her endless supply of ingenuity and inspiration, to Faye for being just genuinely amazing (!), to Charty for her fashion direction and life guidance, Nicki for her help in making me look good, Richard for listening to my constant whining and droning, Angela for covering up all the essential spots and being such a great supporter and listener, to Jake for taking the best photos of me I have seen (in my opinion), and also making a long tiring day seem anything but.

Lastly I would like to thank the three pools of people who help me every day and that is my fans, my friends and my family. My fans for their continual love and support and wonderful moments of clarity, to my friends for their incredible stamina and good humour (which is so important) and to my family for being hugely insane and loving! xxxxx

Will Young

T4 – With a very dodgy 'Father Xmas'

The Brits

These days you only need to sneeze six times in quick succession to be handed an award with 'The World's Best Sneezer' and your name carefully etched on to its base. In 2002 alone there were thousands of award ceremonies which dished out trophies to various deserving recipients. There were the 'Best British Eccentric Awards', won by the inventor of a wickerwork car and a catamaran built from an Edwardian tricycle; 'The Phlemmys' who congratulated realistic scenes of smoking in films and 'The Supreme Flea in Show' – a spin-off of Crufts – that showered with praise a Chihuahua from Wigan for the selection and quality of fleas residing in its hair. However, there are still a few awards that retain a sense

BRITISH BULLDOG!

of gravity and kudos and when it comes to music, there's no ceremony that holds more weight than The Brit Awards. If you're a musician, the foot-tall silver statuettes are an acknowledgement by the music industry that you're actually pretty good at the old music lark (the awards are voted for by an Academy of over 1,000 members from the music industry that includes journalists, retailers and broadcasters).

For Will Young, the run up to the 2003 Brit Awards held mixed emotions. Having been nominated in three categories – Best British Breakthrough Act, Best British Single (for 'Anything Is Possible'/'Evergreen') and Best Pop Act – the 24-year-old was apprehensive about going, and even contemplated 'pulling a sickie' so he wouldn't have to attend the star-studded ceremony at Earl's Court. 'I was beating

Looking through a door in Milan

myself up a bit about having three nominations. I was putting myself down and I don't think I was giving myself any credit at all. I was almost joining the anti-*Pop Idol* people. I needed to give myself some credit. Being nominated for a Brit was something I had always dreamt of and when it happened, I felt as if other people may not think I deserved it and I was in a bit of a fluster about it.' The first thing Will did on hearing the nominations was to go out and buy the albums of his competition in the Best British Breakthrough category, just to see what he would be up against.

'I already had the Ms Dynamite album, but I went out and got The Coral, The Streets and Liberty X. They were all fantastic in their own right. Just being nominated in this category was exciting. This was the one that

Slightly happier looking through a door

Trying to be sexy looking through a door...

From Now On
Album launch

With the gorgeous Emma

Old friends!

I wanted but I really didn't expect to win, I thought it was going to be Ms Dynamite.'

Will thought that if he didn't win an award he would be branded a loser and that his failure would confirm that winning *Pop Idol* was a short-lived career high. He could hear the knives being sharpened. He was also concerned that, even if he was lucky enough to come out on top, he might have to run the gauntlet of perceptions suggesting that he only won on the back of *Pop Idol* 's momentum. He also feared being barracked by the more credible bands attending the event.

'To be honest, I was having quite a testing time. I couldn't win. I didn't want to go at all. I didn't tell anyone I was going to pull a sickie. I was having a really tough time with it. Music is an industry on which everyone has an opinion and lots of people are very passionate about it, which is why they get very heated up. This is a good thing but I always get funny at these kinds of events. You really feel the pressure. It was the biggest event of the year and I didn't want to go. In the end I was honest and told some people that I was thinking of ducking out and they just went, "It will be a really bad idea for you not to go" and they reminded me why I deserved to be there, how hard I'd worked and how much my fans love what I do. The penny dropped: stop being such a wimp and remember what you've achieved.'

Fortunately, Will missed a lot of the build-up to the awards ceremony as he had a month off in Mexico (more on that later), and had an easy return to work by heading off to Italy to do some promotion. Despite feeling chilled out beforehand, on the day itself he admits to being a bag of nerves.

'It was in the car on the way there that the nerves really began to build. I'd got a bottle of Rescue Remedy at the ready and, despite the fact that you are supposed to have just a few drops, I downed it like a shot of tequila! Under the circumstances I was pretty confident! When we arrived I did a few pictures outside, popped to the loo and then went into the main arena. My seat was right at the front, just in front of the audience. And that was brilliant because there was a whole section of Will fans with signs and everything. And that completely calmed me down. I was like, "Oh thank you so much". It was the best thing that could have happened. People often say "the fans pulled me through" and this was a prime example of it being true.'

The Best British Breakthrough Act (previously known as the Best Newcomer, with past winners including Stereophonics and Oasis) was the first award of the night, presented by Sara Cox. Despite what some people might think, the artists aren't craftily told beforehand whether they are going to go home with their bag stuffed with trophies or skulk away empty handed. So when the Radio One DJ read out Will's name it was actual shock written all over his face. 'I think you can tell I was genuinely surprised. I walked down to the stage and was thinking, "Oh f**king hell yes!". I hadn't rehearsed anything to say, but I knew that there were two things I definitely wanted to get into my speech and that was to dedicate it to two of my friends; James who was just going into chemotherapy, and Sarah who had just had an operation for a brain haemorrhage. To be honest that was on my mind and when you find out about things like that, it made me think, "What am I getting nervous about these ceremonies for?" This stuff really is life and death. I have friends who are really ill. In the grand scheme of things this isn't as important as you can make it out to be. James was in the hospital and had just turned on the television as I went, "...and this is dedicated to James" and apparently he jumped up and went, "I've won a Brit". I went to see him the next day, with "the Brit" (which incidentally I didn't let go of for the next 24 hours – it was in my bag, could you imagine if I was caught walking along the street holding on to it?!) As I walked into the hospital he went, "Oh Will you've brought my Brit" and I was like, "I dedicated it to you James, I'm not giving it to you".'

As Will returned to his seat, clutching his award, he admits he started to feel emotional.

'The tears were on the way but I managed to stop them. I was so pleased. It was one of those moments where I looked back and thought, "God, this has

actually been a long hard slog". I was so overwhelmed. I still had the two other awards to go. The worst thing is when they put the cameras on you as they announce the winner. I can't sit there and put on a fake smile. There was a shot of me looking absolutely miserable when Blue won Best Pop Act, but I wasn't at all. I just didn't want to have this big cheesy grin stuck on my face.'

After scooping his award, Will did some interviews. 'We were all on a real high and we decided to play "how many odd words can you get into an interview"... How many people do you know who can get "sausages" into a Brits interview?!'

Then it was time to party.

T4 – Will and Gareth Week with Xmas Cheer

'My record company BMG had a party in Earl's Court, which was held next door to where the ceremony was. As I walked in there were two lines, 50 metres long, of people holding drinks. I said, "Let's go for it". I would have been happy just going from tray to tray! It turned into a very drunken affair. I was on a real high and remember trying to phone all my friends (I didn't phone my parents until the next day as by then it was pretty late and I didn't want to wake them up), screaming down the phone with excitement.' Unlike most revellers who stayed out on the booze all night, the ever-sensible Will broke up his evening with a sneaky trip home. 'My flat was just up the road from Earl's Court and we were going to another party at Home House in Portland Square so I thought, from a self preservation point of view, I should take a break. I don't think my liver would have taken it, so I popped

home and chilled for a bit with some friends. When I arrived at the next party I just sat on the floor with my friends and had a giggle with my management team and people from the record company. In the end I got back home about 5am, I'm sure I wasn't too drunk and falling all over the place but I bet there are photos to the contrary. I tried to get people to come back and carry on the party. I was going, "Now I've got a Brit you will all want to come back and hang out with me" and they were like, "Don't be stupid Will, you're still boring". I thought that was so funny.'

And what did he do with his trophy when he got home?

'I slept holding my Brit like a teddy bear. Isn't that tragic?'

America

You may be the biggest and most popular singer in Britain but there's no guarantee that you'll be successful away from this green and pleasant land, and one of the hardest places to crack is the USA. Many people have tried – Oasis, Robbie Williams, Ronan Keating – but very few have actually succeeded. It's a funny old market, if you're not nu-metal, R'n'B or middle-of-the-road long-haired rockers, you just don't really fit. Back in September 2002, Will had his first taste of America when he was invited to play at the final of *American Idol* which, as with the UK, had been a phenomenal success, drawing an estimated 24 million viewers and making household names of Kelly Clarkson and Justin Guarini. Although he almost arrived in

America with his face a misshapen lump with twigs sticking out of it after a dicey incident with a horse in Costa Rica...

'I went backpacking for a couple of weeks and while I was there I rode a horse for only the second time in my life. I was nervous at first but it seemed ok as I was put on what seemed to be the tamest horse in the world. But then suddenly, out of nowhere, this huge dog appeared and started jumping up at my horse. It must have spooked my ride as it shot off across the beach. I was desperately trying to hang on, being bumped up and down as it galloped across the sand. The next thing I realised we were heading straight for some trees. We ploughed into them and the branches started to slap me around the head. I had the reins in one hand

and was attempting to fend off the leaves with the other. My friend Andy was on the beach and he couldn't see me but all he could hear was this voice drifting out of the trees going, "No, not the face, not the face!! I've got to do *American Idol*!" After that experience I've sworn never to sit on a horse again.'

Thankfully, serious injury was avoided and Will went straight from his holiday on to a plane for America.

'I had kind of missed all of the build-up to the US show so wasn't really sure what I was letting myself in for. At customs the guy was like, "What are you here for?" and I went, "I'm singing on the *American Idol* final" and

INDIAN OCEAN

his reaction made me realise that it was a pretty big show. It was the first time I had been to America and I was really excited. I wasn't under the impression that people would be remotely interested in me at all and I wasn't really sure why I was doing it. But I think Simon Fuller (his manager) was thinking, "Let's give Will a bit of an experience". I can't imagine anyone thought I was going to crack America by appearing on a TV show and singing 'I Get The Sweetest Feeling'.'

Will sang on both *American Idol* shows (the first was when the votes were cast, the second show ran the following night with the result of who had won); along the way he did interviews and mingled with the ten finalists.

Photo shoot in Germany

'I felt like one of those people they bring in for hostage situations! All the TV shows I did I would be introduced like this, "And now we go live over to our expert Will Young. Now Will, what would the contestants be experiencing right now?" It was so funny. I played the real Englishman. I generally stayed out of Justin and Kelly's way because they were right in the middle of it and the last thing they wanted was an English buffoon turning up and interrupting their day.'

After Kelly was announced as the winner, she and Justin faced questions from hundreds of members of the world's press. Unexpectedly, Will was drafted into the press conference too.

Another great polaroid – cafe in Germany

'I couldn't understand, who in America would care? But I thought "in for a penny, in for a dollar" and walked into this massive room full of press. It was like, "Yes he's still here, that British winner, Will Young". When I was announced there was one clap from *Liquid News* or someone (thanks!) It was so absurd I was doing it. Anyway, nobody really wanted to ask me a question so I stood there, pointed and went, "Yes, lady in the blue". She hadn't actually wanted to ask me a question, but I'd always wanted to do that at a press conference!'

While most people in the UK think Mr Young is a well-groomed young man, to the populace of Los Angeles with their obsession with plastic surgery and their warped view of what constitutes beauty, they held a different view and were not shy in making their feelings known.

'I had this lady come up to me and go, "Oh you have great teeth, oh no the top ones are awful". I couldn't believe it. She was so rude it was brilliant. I know that it's the big thing with Americans that they think everyone in England has bad teeth (or was it breath?), but when someone says it to your face you don't know what to say. Then I came back to the UK and was having supper one night in a restaurant in London and this American woman came up to me and said, "If you want to make it in America you've got to change your teeth, it would make you look so much better". So I bit her – not really (I thought about it though!).'

On reflection Will is unsure about whether he will achieve success across the pond (dental work notwithstanding). Of course, that doesn't mean he hasn't got a master plan tucked away inside his brain for cracking the market…

From Now On

On October 7 2002 Will released his debut album *From Now On*. By the end of its first day it had sold 56,000 copies. A week later it had racked up sales of more than 187,000 and it has currently sold over 850,000 copies. The 13 tracks were a mixture of his cover versions – 'Light My Fire', 'Evergreen', 'The Long And Winding Road' – songs written for him; 'Anything Is Possible', 'Lover Won't You Stay', 'You And I', 'Fine Line', 'What's In Goodbye'; and then songs that Will had co-written; 'Side By Side', 'Cruel To Be Kind', 'Over You', 'From Now On' and 'Lovestruck'. Like any musician who has just released their first album, Will wanted an indication of how quickly it was flying off or sticking to the shelves.

'I had a friend who went to HMV and called me going, "I'm here, it's OK they're bulk buying". I said "get off the phone and check out Virgin!"'

The album, recorded in London and Dublin, reached Number One in the charts and received good reviews, even grudgingly good reviews from the more respected music magazines who would have liked nothing better than to rip it to shreds.

'I was really pleased with it. I think it did everything it should have done. I was very nervous putting it out there but then it sold 187,000 in its first week. I know that it wasn't in the same league as, say, Coldplay or Robbie Williams, but it sold pretty well. I thought it was respectable, I felt that there was only so many it could have sold with the fever buying, but then it kept on selling so I started to think, "Actually this could be all right". I didn't read any of the reviews, but I think the gist of it from what I've heard is that it kept people interested and made them think, "OK, the boy's done good – let's see what he comes up with next". I'm pleased they weren't saying, "He's history, pop the champagne".'

However, not all the reviews were glowing, and when one close source to Will questioned its quality, he set the facts straight.

'I had a time when someone was saying, "It could have been a lot better", which I think was unfair in the context of how it was made. It was still made comparatively quickly, plus I had a say in it. It's very mellow and that's what we set out to do, which leaves me free to explore other areas. But for the time that I had to make it, I couldn't have wished for any better. By the end of recording we had quite a few songs and I had supper with Simon at his house and we went through all of the songs and agreed the track listing. We knew we wanted to end on 'Fine Line', because it is a bit of a surprise song and would leave you thinking. There were a few songs that we had to leave off though. Although we left 'Ticket to Love' off, it's had a great response from my fans, so it's not wasted. I kicked off Exeter Festival with it.'

Dutch Idols

The song that Will had most trouble with on the album was 'The Long And Winding Road', a duet with Gareth Gates, which was also his third single. While he had felt comfortable releasing the cover versions of 'Light My Fire' and 'Evergreen', he was uncertain about releasing another world famous song that wasn't his own.

'It was a toughie for me to be honest. My worry with it was it might come across like, "Right, how can we get another hit? I know! We'll combine Gareth fans and Will fans" – I said that at the time. My worry was I'd already covered The Doors and then on the same CD I was doing The Beatles. I was thinking, "Is this taking the piss?" Covers are so difficult to do. If I heard someone do a new version of Joan Armatrading's 'Love And

free flip flops at the 'Dome' in Germany

Affection', which is one of my favourite songs, I probably wouldn't like it just as a matter of course.'

However, despite his reservations Will was happy with the finished result and could understand the reasoning behind doing the song.

'I thought the production on it was great, Steve Lipson (producer) did a great job because there were no thrills, it was just our voices and piano. The video was simple too with the emphasis being on us singing live and in just one take. It did come at a good time, we were both going on tour together and it tied it all up and worked in the context of the show. It was great to see a new generation singing along to a song that I'd first heard 20 years before.'

Will was more excited about the release of the single You And I, which reached number two at the end of November.

'I think that single was a step on – the video, the song and the styling, the whole way we did it. It was the biggest song on the tour by miles. I had so many people come up to me and say that they really liked that particular song. I also think the fact it went to number two was a good thing. If you keep getting number ones all the time you are always going to go downhill at some point, but I needed that to happen to take the pressure off. Christina Aguilera's hit 'Dirrty' was number one and I think that was one of the best songs of last year. I thought, "Right we're not going to get number ones forever, we got that out of the way and now we can move on."'

Charity work

The 'You And I' single held greater significance than just another shiny disc lining the shelves of Woolworths – it was also the official Children In Need single and a chance for Will to give something back to the nation that had voted for him.

'To be honest, I always used to find the programme really annoying and I never really knew what the charity did. So this was a great chance to learn about how much good they do for people. Children In Need helps 400 charities and it was nice to do something for somebody else. When I usually do promotion it's for myself, it's for Will Young, it's for my business

On the news in Italy

– Will Young Incorporated, if you like. One of the first things I did was go to see a project in Newbury for children with hearing disabilities. They were the most wonderful kids I have ever met. They were so well behaved and polite. Lovely. You'd think being in a room with 30 kids would have been full-on, but they were really sweet, it was quite moving, I wanted to stay there the whole day. They were so intelligent. I also visited a women's refuge in London, which takes in women and their children escaping from violent relationships. For me there was a personal interest there because I studied domestic violence at university and did one of my dissertations on the subject. I want people to become irritated because I bang on about it all the time, so I'm going to try to mention it in every interview I do. It will get annoying but at least it will mean it will be getting into people's brains.'

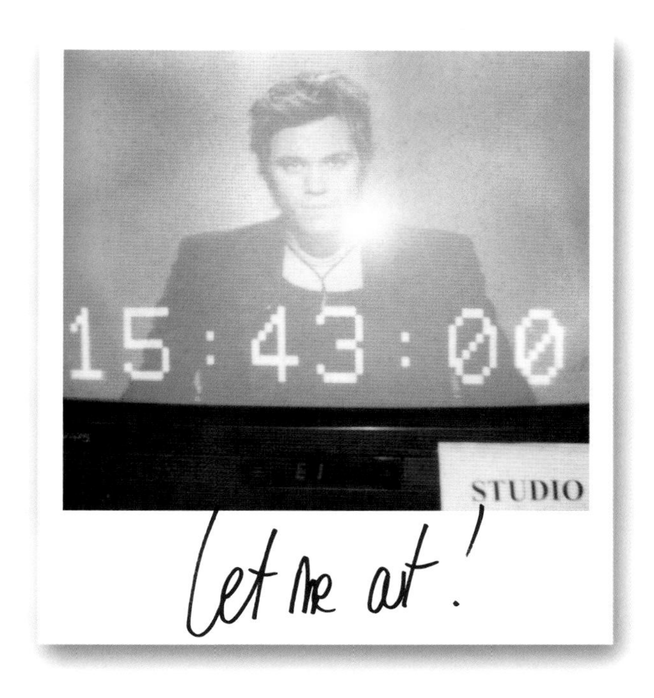
15:43:00
STUDIO
Let me out!

15:44:21
STUDIO
'Trapped'

The day of the actual TV show was a long one for Will, appearing on seven different shows to promote Children In Need, including performances for *Blue Peter* and *The Saturday Show*. It all culminated in him opening the Children In Need programme by singing 'I Get The Sweetest Feeling'. But although the show had begun, Will's night was only just beginning. To help to raise money viewers were given the chance of pledging cash to win a special one-off performance by Will in their own home that night. Needless to say, the phonelines were jammed with callers.

'Eventually there was a winner in Challenge Will and I was flown down to Exeter in a private jet to perform at a girl's house. She was very sweet and lots of her neighbours had come to support me. It all went OK, although it

A very young William @ first Calender shoot

took us ages to get back. We might have flown down in a flash jet, but we had to drive all the way back and didn't get home until five in the morning. That's the stuff you don't see on TV!'

Will's charity work continued when he was made patron of Women's Aid, which gave him the chance to 'irritate' people by doing some interviews where he tried to get into people's brains the widespread problem of domestic violence. However, his plans to promote it in a newspaper went completely awry.

'No one knew I was going to do this, so we'd offered *The Independent* the exclusive. Then, instead of the interview we'd discussed, they ran a piece

about celebrities doing charity work for their own benefit – with me as the prime example. I was livid. They'd given me the impression we were going to produce a positive article together, but nothing of the sort happened. If they had actually taken the time to talk to me properly, they would have found out that I could discuss the subject eloquently and at length. I didn't just pick a charity by going, "Oh women, there's an audience, I should choose that subject to show I'm sensitive and sell more records".

I was trying to do something I believe in and got completely shot down for it. I didn't do it to promote a single or for myself, it was 100% for Women's Aid. I was extremely disappointed.'

A little friend I met in Holland

Will had a better time when he was the guest on Radio One's *Sunday Night Surgery*, hosted by Emma B and Dr Mark Hamilton. It gave him the chance to impart advice and try to help the listeners with their problems.

'It was one of the most chilled out things I've done. I'm interested in that type of thing because I used to want to be a counsellor. I seem to know people and situations and have always been able to help people.' That particular show was based around domestic violence so before going on, Will read through his old revision papers and made key notes so he would be well prepared.

'I hate the idea that people can live through their whole life and never be empowered, they live an existence where they are bullied and are miserable.

If you can empower yourself it is the most wonderful thing in the world. There are people who are in these situations where their life is terrible but they don't feel they can do anything about it. Someone wrote into the programme and said, "How can I leave? I have no qualifications, I have kids, I can't get a job, I have no money. If I leave it's going to be really s**t and even though I get beaten s**tless every day, my kids do get new clothes and they wouldn't have that if I left". And on one hand you can't answer this as you are not in their shoes. However you can assure them that by empowering themselves and leaving behind a life of continual misery and ritual humiliation, you can realise a life of safety and security and most importantly find your happiness – and this is what charities like Women's Aid do and why they are set up. There is a way out, however distant it seems, and I believe that everyone experiencing violence in their life in whatever form, is entitled to that."

Although the programme covered such a serious subject, there were a few lighter moments.

'This 17 year-old guy called in saying that he'd slept with his girlfriend's brother and asked what he should do. I tried to make him feel at ease by saying, "You're lucky – I was trying to sleep with my sister's boyfriends for ages". The newspapers picked up on it and ran stories about how I was trying to sleep with my sister's boyfriend – come on!! But I thought that the *Surgery* was great. There are so many people who are in a pickle. I remember when I was younger I didn't have anybody to talk to and I could have done with it. Young people need lifelines and I think the situation is a lot better these days. But when I was growing up and having thoughts about being gay, as I knew I was from an early age, I don't remember seeing any numbers up on boards or anyone giving a talk about it at school. That's why I think programmes like that are very worthwhile and the plethora of questions was amazing. It made me think, "Bloody hell, I thought I had problems but what a normal life I actually lead!"'

The Tour

'I was bloody nervous.' Now, you might have cottoned on to the fact that Will isn't somebody who confidently strides through life completely fearless, he has times when his self-esteem and belief in his ability are low. The Will & Gareth tour, which saw the duo, supported by their old *Pop Idol* friend Zoe Birkett, sell out venues in London, Birmingham, Manchester, Glasgow and Newcastle, was another time when the Young nerves would start to jangle.

'I was nervous because I thought people would be expecting to hear my new songs and to be honest the album wasn't really a stadium album,

Sharing a joke with the gorgeous Zoe

it was more mellow and more Burt Bacharach than rousing, foot-stomping pop. I was worried that the music just wouldn't go down well.'

Will's jitters were relieved by the fact that this time around he would be performing with a live band. And more importantly for Will, the band contained musicians that he had worked with consistently over the past year and with whom he had built up something of a rapport.

'I knew most of them fairly well and it was such a great feeling to be getting up every day and going to rehearsals with a live band. I felt it was another step up to where I wanted to be. The band has been just amazing for me and has done a hell of a lot subconsciously. To be on stage with

those guys, who are undeniably cool, really does something to you. They brought so much to the show. They did little things like putting in Stevie Wonder licks that I wouldn't have thought of and were so cool. There's nothing better than singing with a live band.'

However, the tour didn't start well for Will as the night before the first date at the London Arena he was up until the early hours filming the video for the 'You And I' single. He was shattered, but after a few a hours sleep he was ready to go.

'Right before the tour there were a lot of distractions. Gareth and I both had promotion to do for 'The Long And Winding Road' single, I was doing

Tired

Awake

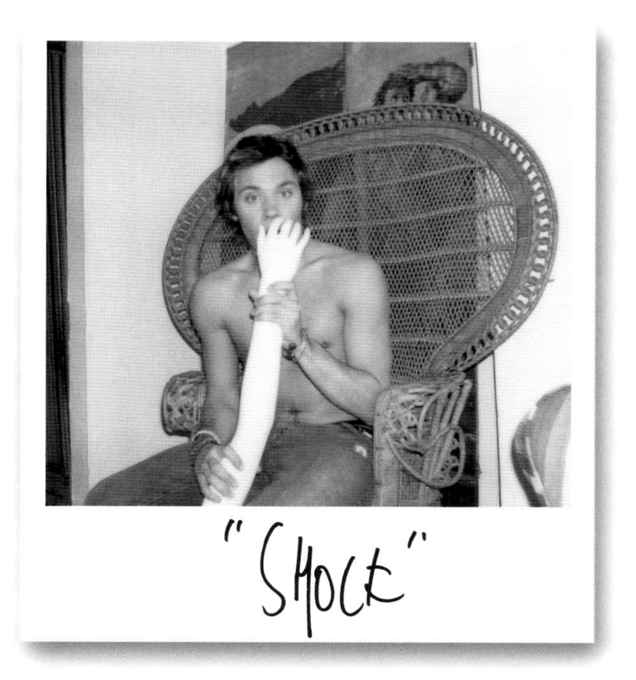

a spokesman said....
......"I'm shocked!"

Warming up in Holland

promotion for the album and then promotion for the tour. It was bloody tiring. I couldn't wait to get out of London, because I like being in the bubble of the tour and when you are in the city there are just too many distractions. I enjoy being on the bus because you are suddenly in this mad world where nothing else matters but the tour. I like the regularity of it. You wake up and go to a new place, you do the gig, go out and party, go to sleep, wake up, go to a new place, do the gig and so on. It's very self-contained. The 'You And I' video was from 6am to 3am the night before we started. That was literally the only time I had in my schedule to fit it in. Sometimes, when it's really mad, you get to the stage where there is no time at all for anything. There just isn't "a good time". So you just have to fit things in where you can. I was on a real anti-everyone by the start of the

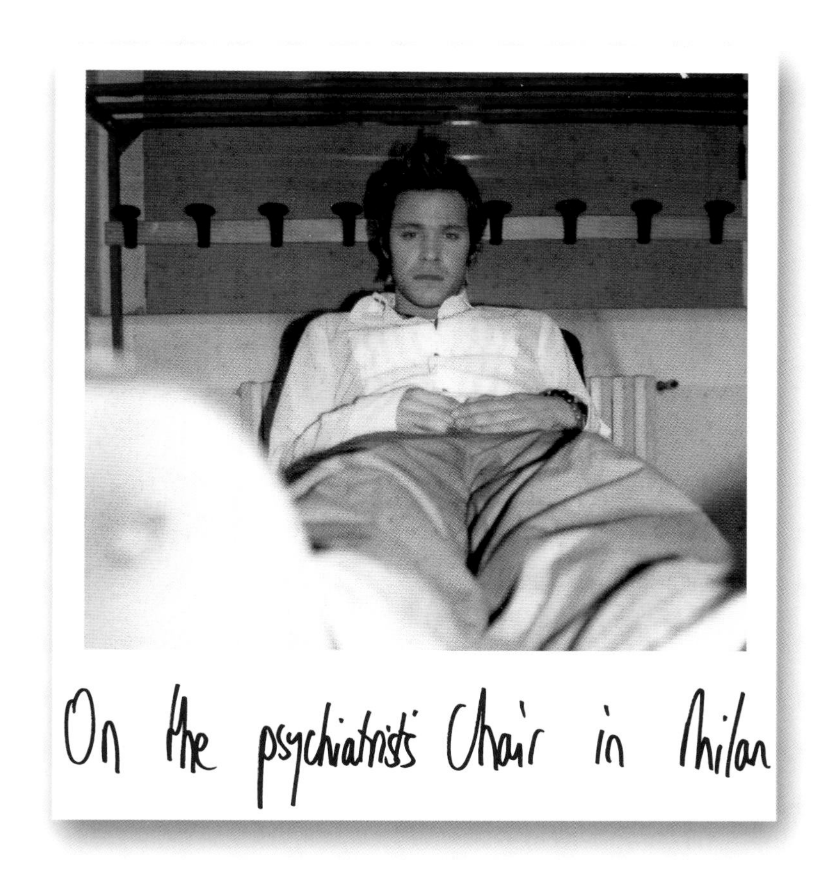

On the psychiatrist's Chair in Milan

tour, not in a nasty way, but I just wanted to be on stage singing and wanted to leave all the other stuff behind.'

Will's feelings were exacerbated by the presence of a film crew, who were there to shoot reportage footage of the boys in rehearsals, which would then make up part of the tour's DVD.

'I'm really bad with filming while I'm rehearsing. I got pissed off with myself afterwards when I watched the DVD because I'm being crap. Those bits in rehearsals and backstage are really good to see and are quite funny. So it was unprofessional that I didn't give it my very best. At the time I felt the filming was getting in the way of me doing my job, but then when I look

back at it, it's really good and they did a great job with the footage. Bless them for putting up with me.'

Despite the mad pre-tour rush, the congested rehearsals and the large dollops of anxiety, the 500,000 fans who came clutching their 'I love Will' signs (and other slightly more risqué slogans) went away happy.

'My set was quite intimate. I had an idea to start with 'Ain't No Sunshine' – Gareth and I were very involved in all aspects of the tour right from the beginning. We were consulted on things like stage design, which was great. When I was on holiday in Costa Rica I had loads of ideas, one of them being that I wanted to start singing beneath the stage so the audience would hear me before they could see me. I didn't want a big flashy entrance, I wanted it to be quite understated.'

Will's favourite moments from the tour include singing 'You And I' – 'I thought that was the real showstopper' – the fact that his voice didn't fall apart; 'I'd listened a lot to my voice coaches David and Carrie Grant and it stayed strong, in fact it was at its strongest during the final two performances'; and his duets with Zoe and Gareth.

'One night I was doing the duet with Zoe and we both had to walk down these stairs. She turned to look at me and I wasn't there – I'd completely lost my footing and I was frantically trying to lie back on the stairs in a sexy way, to make out that it was all part of the show. But you could see in her eyes she was like, "What are you doing?!" One of my other favourite moments was the duet with Gareth, as we would do this on a "B" stage which we would walk out on and it meant that all the people who had seats right at the back of the arena – who probably thought they were going to be miles away from us – were now in the front seats and had the best view. I thought that was really important.'

Of course, Will being Will, he did have some doubts about his performance and admits he thought there were times where he resembled a well-known, clean-cut, virginal crooner – "I did think I looked like Cliff Richard!"

Good Soundcheck

With the tour over, it was rapidly approaching Christmas and he was invited to perform at a special carol concert in aid of the Nordoff Robbins charity at St. Luke's church in London.

'In the past they had the likes of Annie Lennox and Robbie Williams perform so I was pretty chuffed to be asked. Plus, I've always wanted to sing in a church.'

As happens at any event Will attends, there were a cluster of photographers outside and, rather than cause a fuss, Will stayed in his car out of the way, until the last moment.

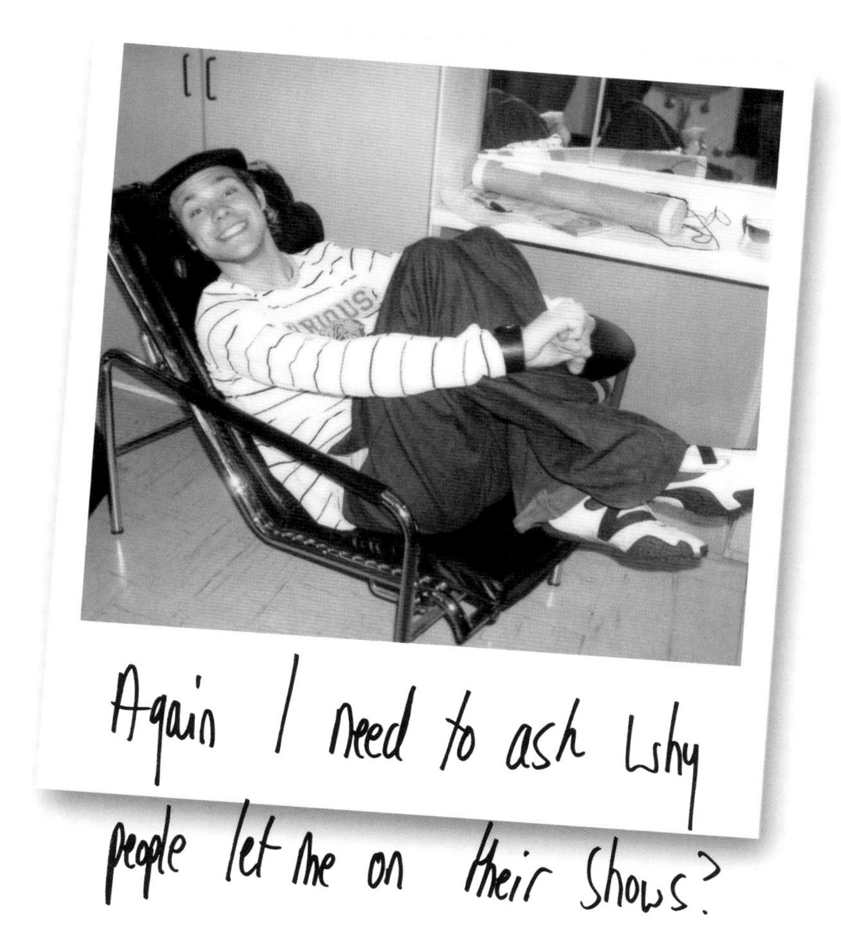

'They said they'd tell me when they were ready and I thought I would walk in when people were still milling around waiting to sit down, but I strolled in and everyone was seated and all the people, about a thousand I reckon, turned to look at me. My seat was right down the front and I was wearing a pair of very clicky shoes. I was so embarrassed. You can see how some stars get the reputation for being a bit of a diva, but I didn't know everyone would be waiting for me. I had eight friends sitting with me in the same row and as I sat down they all turned to me and went, "You w**ker!" It was like being back at school, sitting in the chapel and trying not to laugh.'

Although Will attended a Catholic school and was eager to sing in a church, he admits that he's not really a big religious person. However, he admits

finding true love @ Munich Airport

He's my perfect match –
quiet, dependable, consistent.....

.... We even shared jokes. It broke my heart when I had to fly home

that recently he has started to think more deeply into what this funny old life really means.

'I do have my beliefs. I think the *Pop Idol* experience was a big spiritual thing for me. I don't like to talk about it that much because I think it's a personal thing. The last year and a half I have become a lot more spiritual in trying to find reasons for things. Where did this voice come from? I'm really lucky, but why am I lucky that I do a job that I love? Where did that come from? It does makes you think a bit more.'

The carol concert marked the last thing in Will's diary before Christmas and after his non-stop schedule he was glad of the yuletide break.

Dolce & Gabbana outfit for Festivalbar

'I did way too much Christmas shopping, but I love buying presents for people. I had a day shopping with a friend and we had a car to take us round London, which was great fun. By the time it got to Christmas I was bored of seeing my face in the mirror so everyone else must have been bored of me, I seemed to be on every TV show. I thought, "Right, I need to get off the TV and stop boring people with me."'

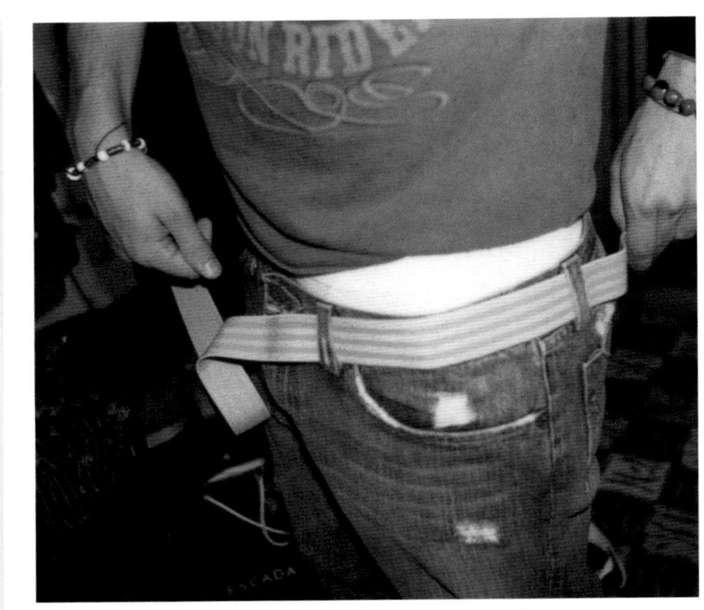

Dresden Hilton : Photoshoot

The Royal Variety Show

Since King George V and Queen Mary in 1912 fancied a bit of a knees-up one evening, The Royal Variety Performance has been a regular big night out in the entertainment calendar (apart from during the World Wars when the royal family were in mourning). It's a chance for a unique collection of dancers, singers, comedians, puppeteers, magicians and general household names to gather to raise money for the Entertainment Artistes' Benevolent Fund. For someone who has dominated the business in 2002, it was no surprise that Will was invited to open the show.

Warm ups @ the Dome

Will wasn't the only member of the Young clan there that evening – his brother Rupert was working at the show looking after Kylie Minogue. This meant, of course, that Will got to meet her too – 'She's lovely. Very small, very beautiful and a great little bottom. A real pro.' As well as singing, Will was asked to return to the stage to introduce a few of the night's acts.

'Literally no one laughed at my jokes. I'm sure when they showed it on the television they had to add laughter in! After I did 'Live And Let Die' I came back on to introduce a ventriloquist and they had this script that I was supposed to follow, but I just ignored it and went, "Now some people like to go running, some people play tiddlywinks, a minority of the country likes to stuff their hands up the backsides of puppets. Now the majority of these

Always make friends with the local police

people get arrested and the minority appear on the Royal Variety Show, here's your first act". I thought I was hysterical and had a little laugh at my own joke, but no one else did!'

As Prince Charles tapped his highly polished shoe to Anastasia, Kylie, Gareth Gates and Shania Twain, backstage Will was more interested in meeting up with one of the elder statesmen of British light entertainment.

'I got to meet Bob Monkhouse. There was something about him that warmed me to him. He really reminded me of my grandfather and I felt very protective of him. I was thinking, "This guy is really quite important and you should give him respect". For the big finale I found I was standing

Stuffing my face @ Calendar Shoot

The new Calendar..
... a good day @ the office!

next to him on stage and he had confetti all over him and I thought, "I don't want him to meet Prince Charles with confetti all over him" so I was picking it out of his hair, and we had a really nice chat. While Prince Charles was at one end working his way down the line, Bob turned to me and said, "I think you are a very funny man, I saw you on Graham Norton's show and I thought you were great", and I said, "Well, coming from you that's a real compliment". He seemed very wise and I was really touched by him. I wrote him a letter after the event saying how pleased I was to meet him and just checking that he was OK. I hope he got it.'

Acting

There was one last thing that 2002 held in store for Will. Before he could 'stop boring people with his face' as he puts it, an opportunity came up that he just couldn't turn down – the chance to act in a West End play. Since November 2001, the comedy *The Play Wot I Wrote* had been consistently drawing rave reviews at the Wyndham's Theatre. Directed by Shakespearean thesp Kenneth Branagh and based around a tribute to seventies comedians Eric Morecambe and Ernie Wise, the three-man show – starring Sean Foley, Hamish McColl and Toby Jones – would have a special guest star every week for its finale. The likes of Ralph Fiennes, Kylie Minogue, Jude Law, Ewan McGregor and Roger Moore had all

previously graced the stage as a be-wigged eighteenth-century count in the final act.

'I went to see the play with my friend Pilky and I was secretly hoping that they might know that I was there and would ask me to be in it! We were passed a message inviting us to go backstage, but I never do that – why should you be allowed to hang around backstage just because you are vaguely famous? But then they called up my management company and asked if I would like to do it. It was quite a big script, it wasn't just a few lines and I am very bad at line learning. I discovered that in the only term I studied acting at university. I'm not saying that I'm funny but in the very little acting I've done I've found caricatures and comedy acting much easier to do than straight stuff. I was scared about

Me singing to myself

doing it, because I knew I could make a fool out of myself, but I'd seen the play, knew what it was all about and what I was letting myself in for. I hoped that people who went to see it would say to their friends afterwards, "And the special guest was Will Young and do you know what? He was really good in it".'

The role meant intensive rehearsals and memorising the many pages of script, but Will found it relaxing and a completely different atmosphere to that of his recent tour.

'What I loved about it was that it was a very different feeling to singing. I learnt to really control an audience when I'm on stage. It's all about timing and the one look that you can give. You make a joke, there's a silence and

Squash in Holland

you can keep the laughter going by just giving one look which gets another laugh. I did two nights and I would have done a week without question. I loved it. They were such nice guys and bloody hell they work hard. The best thing is you can muck it up and that would be a joke and they would run with it for five minutes before they returned to the script. The first time I appeared I would make myself laugh as the director said that was the best thing to do, if you laugh at them sending you up, it shows you don't mind them taking the piss and allows the audience to relax into it.'

As well as remembering not to say the name of the Scottish play (it's bad luck to mention *Macbeth* in a theatre!), Will learnt one more important acting tradition.

Hello Bottom!

Photo shoot in Holland

quello sporco, onesto sbirro !
UNA DISTRIBUZIONE COLUMBIA PICTURES
DINO DE LAURENTIIS
presenta
AL PACINO in
ERPICO"
MIKIS THEODORAKIS
PETER MAAS pubblicato in Italia dalla Rizzoli Editore
WALDO SALT E NORMAN WEXLER
IDNEY LUMET
Intermaco S.p.A.

Caught on Camera

'In the dressing room you wrote a message on the wall to the next special guest doing the play. Scribbled on the wall were messages from Jude Law to Charles Dance and Charles Dance to Simon Callow. It was mad. I had to write a note to Miranda Richardson saying, "Dear Countess Toblerone. Please ignore what you have read in the papers, I am indeed your straight husband and I love you lots", and then in brackets I put, "Actually I do really love you".'

While at Exeter University Will performed in three musicals, including the lead in *Oklahoma*, and still considers acting to be something he would like to move into at some point in his career.

'Originally I was going to go to acting school from prep school. But I didn't have that much confidence in my acting. I would love to have done Shakespeare. I did a short film at uni, it's dreadful, it's called *University of Life* and was shot in the form of a mockumentary. Plus I did a comedy sketch thing at school which I wrote and directed, it was a leaving present for a teacher who was going. It was a nice send-off, although I'm not sure he appreciated it as all it did was take the piss out of him. And even if I do say so, it is still bloody funny.'

He's also set his sights on appearing in another musical, although it would need to be the right project.

'I'd love to do one when the time is right. I would like to do it when my career is established. Sometimes people only do a musical when their career is on the down slope and everyone is going, "Oh where are they now? Oh, they're only doing musicals". But I think musicals are a really hard thing to do. Ultimately, I would like to do this musical film idea that's been knocking around. I've seen an idea that's really interesting and I haven't gone for it yet, but I will soon and I think it will be really cool. I'd want to do something original rather than a reworking of an old favourite which seems to be so prevalent in the West End at the moment.'

And then there is Will's grand ambition. Picture the scene: Her Majesty's finest secret service agent James Bond strolling along in a tuxedo, before swivelling

A necessary part of the kit: make up!

to fire a bullet at the camera as Will's voice reverberates around the cinema. Yup, Will wants to follow in the footsteps of Shirley Bassey, Duran Duran, Tina Turner and Madonna and record the next 007 theme tune.

'I would love it to be a big John Barry production and, more importantly, I would get to do a cameo as a jazz singer in some club that James Bond walks into. We can but dream I suppose.'

If the producers of the next Bond film have any foresight, they would sign him up now!

Will's big month off

Everyone needs a holiday, and if you had had a 2002 like Will – full of competition, intense public scrutiny, recording, record releases, tours and promotion – you would have been in desperate need of one. As soon as Will had finished *The Play Wot I Wrote*, he was on vacation. No more interviews, no more TV appearances and a whole month to get some serious 'R and 'R.

'To Simon Fuller's credit he was the one who said, "Have a big break" – he read me like a book and knew that I needed it. I don't think I would have asked for it. I decided right from the start that I would plan my holiday out so that I wouldn't waste it. So after spending New Year in Cornwall with friends, I went to Paris for a few days. I just pottered *en France* and bought some things for my house – an old chopping board for £10, antique champagne glasses £80 for 12 – brilliant.'

However, it's not easy for Will to just switch off. As soon as he wasn't dashing around from job to job he had time to think about where his career was going and how he wanted it to progress.

'I got really psyched up about the next album. I started to send lots of emails at about 2am, I was worried that everyone in the office would think I had gone mad as they suddenly had this barrage of emails going, "What's going on here? I want do to this. How about working with these writers? I've listened to this album and what about this producer? Let's do this TV show." I was just very motivated. I was having mad ideas. I wanted to know if people were pushing my boundaries. I love it when I'm motivated as I like to feel I'm doing the most I can do with my life. When you take time off you get so inspired. I had so many ideas.'

The work didn't even stop when Will headed off to Mexico for two weeks to catch up on some sun, sea, sand and ...and speaking into a Dictaphone.

Mexican chic

Mexico

A lovely photo

'I had so many ideas, I took a little recorder with me so I could tape all my thoughts. Although near the end of the holiday it broke so I had to resort to phoning up my mobile from my hotel to record a song I'd just come up with. When I got home I listened to it and just thought, "I must have been drunk that evening" because it was terrible.'

Will's time in Mexico was a throwback to his days spent backpacking as a student, and although he did afford himself a few nights living it up in a luxurious hotel, the rest of the time he and his friends, Claire and Hugh, slept in hostels like any other normal young group of holidaying friends.

'When I go away I make a point of backpacking and staying in youth hostels. Of course it's nice to stay a couple of days in a bit of luxury, but it makes you realise you really are not very important because back in England you can get trumped up about yourself. I don't realise how on-duty I am when I'm here. For instance, if I'm walking past a restaurant I will think, "I wonder if anyone is looking out going, 'Hey there goes Will Young'" and I don't mean that in an arrogant way but you do become very conscious of yourself.'

Although even if you go as far afield as Central America, there's no guarantee you'll not bump into a party of holidaying Brits, as Will found out one boozy night.

'It was my birthday while we were away so we went to a bar for a few drinks and they had a salsa band. After consuming a lot of cocktails I got up and sang 'Light My Fire', but then they relegated me to backing singer because they thought I wasn't good enough – haha. I couldn't believe it. But then they let me sing 'Moondance', which I didn't know any of the words for apart from 'Moondance'. There were a group of English air hostesses next door and they were sitting having a drink and heard me sing and went, "Wait a minute, that sounds like Will Young" they came round the corner and were like "Oh my god, it *is* Will Young". There I was, completely trashed, singing with this salsa band. To top the night off as we stumbled home we came, completely out of nowhere, upon this random kebab house. We pigged out, big time. In the end I had about seven weeks off and I felt my working year didn't really start until February.'

Repair Works

Big in Italy

Will had already had a taste of promoting his singles abroad when he visited the USA. But on his return to work in February, the international push began in earnest. The first European destination to be treated to the singing delights of Mr Young was Italy where his single 'Light My Fire' went straight to number two in the airplay charts.

'During the UK tour we had this big bus-load of people from Europe come up to Birmingham to see the show. They each had a pack about me and Gareth, with our videos and our music in a nice little box. It was very impressive. Out of all the different countries' representatives who came

Preparing for the off

to see us, it was Italy who really went for me, which was great because I love Italy. They saw me and said, "This guy looks great and sounds great". Out there, as well as just doing the usual magazines, I also did style magazines like Italian *Vogue* and *L'Huomo Vogue*. I was coming in at all angles. It was strange because suddenly I was really enjoying singing 'Light My Fire', which, when you look at it, was my original tune which was turned around on *Pop Idol*. Beforehand I hadn't really given myself any credit for the way I had sung it. They don't have *Pop Idol* in Italy, so the single just had to stand alone and was completely out of that context. I watched the video, which I hadn't done in a long time, and thought, "Actually, that's a bloody good video and I'm really proud of that cover".'

In Italy, Will spent five days in Milan and Rome to promote his single. While in the country's capital he got to mingle with Hollywood film stars and Italy's coolest up-and-comers, that you just had to be seen with (darhling!).

'While I was in Rome I did a shoot with the Italian actress Maria Grazia Cucinotta, who was in the Bond film *The World Is Not Enough*. She was absolutely gorgeous and one of the nicest ladies I've ever met. She came all the way from France to do this shoot with me.'

After all the hoo-ha surrounding *Pop Idol* in the UK and being unable to go out for a stroll without being spotted, it has been a strange feeling for Will to go to countries where he is completely unknown.

'You turn up and there are no fans there and you suddenly realise that you have got used to them being there all the time. It's really good for your ego and makes you understand that in the grand scheme of things you are a complete nobody. I've come to appreciate what 99 per cent of artistes have to go through when they are just starting out on their careers. I'm the lucky one per cent who hasn't had to stand up on a stage and face a room full of people who have never heard of you and go, "This is my music".'

He's also released material in Holland and Germany (his single 'You And I' went to number two in Holland) and has been frequently heading back and forth to promote his singles there.

INDIAN OCEAN

'Germany is a huge market. I have to admit the first time I went there I wasn't in the best of moods because I was feeling very homesick. I got a really late flight and didn't get there until 11pm and then had to get up early the next morning.'

A mixture of tiredness, homesickness and a lack of understanding of the way the press was conducted in Germany meant Will had an inauspicious start there.

'I was appearing on a big music show called *The Dome* and while I was there I was booked to do a photo shoot. When I got there I saw where the shoot was to be held – it was literally a little roped-off section of the canteen.

They were wheeling pop stars in and wheeling them out. And the worst thing was that they all looked the same. I suddenly thought, "My god, I'm a robot". I just thought "I must exterminate, exterminate!". After a quick battery change, I got my act together and realised how important it was to do this type of thing. After that the rest of the trip was great, I did more photo shoots and interviews and they all went fine.'

Just like Italy, Will enjoys the time he spends in the Netherlands. He finds their attitude to life a lot more laid back and easy-going, something he can relate to.

'I think the Dutch are really cool. I find the press a lot easier and they don't care about sexuality. It's not an issue and you realise how much it

People having fun on Queen's Day

is an issue here in England. I visited Amsterdam during the Queen's Day celebrations and it's amazing. Everywhere you look is a sea of orange. It's like the biggest party you have ever seen. I did a performance on a stage that was positioned slap bang in the middle of the street. There were so many people there. Unfortunately the music to 'Light My Fire' didn't start so I was standing up there with nothing to sing. I went, "Has anyone got a beer?" and people started throwing up their glasses. It was really funny. After the gig we went to The Supper Club which is this strange restaurant where everyone eats their dinner on these huge beds. Every night there's a set course and you eat your starters wearing plastic surgery gloves.'

William having fun on Queen's Day

A big concern for Will about performing on the continent was that he would be forced to mime rather than sing live on some of the TV shows. It's something he has never done.

'I won't mime because I can sing, and I was told that if I go to do promotion in Europe I would have to. There have been times in England where I've been asked to mime and I have been like, "I can't believe you have asked me to do that?" I would feel like an idiot miming and would probably forget my words. One of the great things about Italy and Holland was the amount of acoustic promotion I did. The first thing I did in Holland was *MTV Unplugged*, which for me was amazing. I did three songs in this bar and it's done in such a way that if the people in the crowd are not interested then they just turn

away and have a drink. So I was determined to make them put down their drinks and listen, and they did.'

Although Will is happy about doing European press, there is one country where he would rather he wasn't shifting records by the ferry-load.

'My family has always gone on holiday to France and it's where I escape to. So what would happen if I suddenly became big there? Where would I go to escape then? Of course, being a success worldwide would be amazing but I don't like the idea of not being able to go to places and just be a normal person.'

The new album

The famous screenwriter William Goldman once said, 'Everyone knows what has been successful yesterday. But nobody knows what's going to be successful tomorrow.' It's a thought that has been going through Will's head since he started work on his new album.

'When I made the first album I thought, "Could I be a songwriter? Could I be a pop star?" But now I have been thinking more along the lines of, "What sort of songwriter am I? What sort of singer am I?" (oh, and... "can I still be a popstar?!"). I went back and looked at all the songs I picked on the show which were soulful classics or jazzy blues. That's the sort of thing I do and that's why people like me. I don't do acid funk or rocky pop. But I had a chat with my father who said, "Well wouldn't it be awful if it all went wrong and you hadn't done what you really thought you should be doing. Just be who you are." I agreed. The great thing is that Simon, my manager, has let me grow as a writer. You would not expect that my last single was in November and it's now October and I haven't released a single. I think Simon has seen that I have needed this year to grow and experiment and in a way to do all the things I haven't

Working hard Writing (text messages) in Ireland

really had a chance to do to date. It has been great to have a chance to sit back from the work I had been doing for a bit and concentrate on finding more of a sound that defines Will Young.'

This time around Will has been working again with some of the same writers he built up a good rapport with on his first album – Biff and Jules, for example – but has also been experimenting with new musicians and songwriters so that the collection of songs he has are much more varied.

'I have really worked with some varied writers this year and I feel in a way that this is what this year has been all about. It has been fun

working with so many different people – they all differ artistically, but it is also a challenge to meet and create a working artistic environment with so many different people on a week to week basis.'

Will has worked with the likes of Jonathon Shorten – who penned much of Gabrielle's last album – as well as a writer he was keen to work with called Eg White, who has worked with one of Will's favourite artists, Emiliana Torrini.

'It was great to work with Jonathon and Eg. I had heard of Jonathon from Gabrielle's album *Rise* and we got on really well. He is a real musician who comes up with great grooves and it was refreshing to be writing

from such fresh sounds. Eg has been a real joy to work with. I was a huge fan of his work with Emiliana Torrini as I am very keen on her style of music – and Eg and I hit it off from day one. The great thing is that everyone works differently and whether you create a song through a lyric or a melody idea, by jamming away or through a more methodical approach, the outcome can always be spectacular! (Sometimes it can be awful too... but such is the creative process!).'

There have also been people writing especially for Will, one of them being Karen Poole, of whom Will is very fond and for whom he predicts a big future.

'We worked together on a great song which is very jazzy and we really hit it off from the start. She has become a huge writer writing for the likes of Janet Jackson and Kylie and I am really chuffed that she is writing for the album. It is important if you are singing other people's songs that you connect with them or else you can never perform them with any sense of belief. I feel that Karen gets me as a singer and as a performer and hence the songs she writes I believe in instantly.'

It's not just UK-based writers that Will has worked with; in July he returned to America.

'I was writing in Florida for ten days and then spent ten days in Los Angeles. I really felt that having taken a whole year to grow and fully experience the writing process, America simply had to be a part of it. We put together a list of people whom we all felt would be good to work with and then off we went! The writer I was most excited about meeting was a man called Robin Thicke, whom I am a big fan of. He is an American singer/songwriter/producer and his music really is incredible. I knew that musically he would be inspirational to work with and it really turned out that way. We could have written a whole album within a month!'

As well as Robin Thicke, Will hooked up with Steve Morales (of Enrique Iglesias fame), Lester Mendez (Santana and Jewel) and Rick Nowels (Texas to Dido). Did he enjoy his three weeks in the land of opportunity? 'I'll definitely be going back soon!'

One of the biggest changes this time around has been the lyrics that Will has been writing. He wanted to take them on a step and write more from the heart than he did before.

'Lyrics are what I was initially insecure about and I remember people saying to me that on the last album they were a bit boring. I felt I had to believe in them this time round. I've tried to put a lot more of me into

No photos please

The winning moment (repeated in Holland)

them, my experiences and the things that have gone on around me. The best example I can give is a song called 'Take Control'. I got a letter from a lady who's in a violent relationship and I burst into tears when I read it. It was the most beautifully written letter I've ever read. Her vulnerability upset me and I was cross because there was nothing I could do as she didn't leave any way of contacting her. So I wrote that song for her.'

He may possess the voice of an angel, but Will admits he won't be sitting down behind a piano and tinkling the ivories on stage any time soon.

'My piano playing is not very good, although I am getting one for my new house. I'm learning the tambourine at the moment, which is a lot harder than people might think! I want to learn a wind instrument as well and I'm considering the trumpet. I took lessons for a year when I was 13 and I want to do that again.'

Of course Will can work with the best writers around, pen some of the most heartbreaking lyrics and lay down some of the finest vocals ever recorded, but there's no guarantee that his new album will receive a glowing review.

'Deep down I'm a bit concerned, I suppose. If people slate it, I'll feel hurt. If it's voted "Album of the month" I'll be ecstatic. This time I would like the good reviews. Last time, even if it was a generally good review, I'd think, "Oh that's just because they have to say that because it will sell a lot because of *Pop Idol*". But this time round I've lived this album, there has been nothing else going on in my life but this – and if it gets slated I'll be gutted. My dad said to me, "You do your best and if you can say 100 per cent that that's me, there's nothing more you can do". He's clever, my dad.'

Another big change in Will's career has been his publishing deal with Sony, which means that they now own the rights to the songs that he writes.

'There are a lot of opportunities. I see it as a two-way thing. To begin with there were a lot of publishing companies interested in signing my deal. But I'd made up my mind right at the beginning that I was going to talk to Sony, because I really trust them and it was where I did my work experience when I was at uni. So I'm basically now signed to the two people I was assisting at Sony. When I was doing work experience there, they actually offered me a job but it would have meant leaving university. My dad was saying I should take the job, but I felt I had to finish my course. You don't get those jobs that quickly or easily and I knew that I would have really landed on my feet. I would sit at my desk and look through 200 CVs a day from people who wanted to be in the industry and I couldn't believe I was turning the job down.'

Fate just had something more grand in store for Will.

Fitness

Believe it or not, Will doesn't keep his boyish good looks or healthy physique by spending his free time slumped on the sofa eating a huge mound of cakes. But neither is he a fitness fanatic who studiously scrutinises the calorie content of everything he eats and blows out his cheeks pumping an inordinate amount of iron for five hours at a time. What he does do is run. And, like Forrest Gump, he does rather a lot of it.

'I was always very keen on sport at school, particularly running and the 400 metres. And when I got to university I had the option of joining the

More stretching!

athletics club or joining the acting club and you either did one or the other. I think that's the case with everything as you get older – you narrow your options and focus in on one thing. You have to start letting things go. Proper running was one of the things I let go. Running keeps me strong minded. Because of an evening you don't want to race around a track, your body is going, "What the hell are you doing" and your mind is doing the same thing so you have to force yourself to do it. I love racing – I'm really quite competitive. It was always my dream to go to the Olympics and run in the 400 metres. I always believed I could do it. I used to run it in sub-50 seconds at school and in the Olympics the times are around 43 seconds. I know I was a long way off, but I would have liked to have given it a go.'

Running gives him a chance to clear his head and not think about the good or bad things that have happened to him that day.

'I tend to do mostly aerobic exercise, I'm not a big pumping iron kind of man, because I build muscle really easily so I don't want to end up looking like some sort of man mountain. By the end of the day my mind is so full of things, I'll be either massively happy about one thing or massively stressed about another, so running takes my mind off those things. It's a time when I can switch off.'

Will had a chance to show his competitive edge in May when he took part in a six-mile charity run to raise money for Capital Radio's Help

You don't get more random than a inflatable giant mouse on a lamppost in Germany

A London Child in Hyde Park. And out of the 5,400 runners, 300 of them from amateur running clubs, he finished 22nd with a time of 39 minutes and 22 seconds (round of applause!!).

'I heard about it from my friend Mary at Capital Radio. I wanted to do the run to motivate me to keep on going to the gym and I knew if I was doing it I wouldn't want to look unfit in front of the public. I aimed to do it in 50 minutes. I like raising money for good causes and being able to do it through something I really enjoy too. It was great!'

Although Will keeps himself fit, he still had to hit the running machines and build up his stamina so that he wouldn't face the embarrassment of trundling in last.

'I started by going to the gym and running the course on the machine for six weeks then I started actually doing the route in Hyde Park. When I turned up the other runners probably thought "Bloody pop star". I didn't go off too quickly but managed to maintain a good pace. The last two kilometres were very difficult but I was helped by lots of people around the course shouting encouragement at me. I was so pleased with my time and hopefully I surprised people. It's good to throw people off guard and keep them guessing. I like the idea they are going, "Ok we thought we had worked him out, but now he does a run and he's quite good at it, what is he about?" I don't like to be a one dimensional person.'

Not all of the runners, though, were impressed with Will's running attire.

'I had on this pair of bright yellow and blue rugby socks. One runner went by going, "Why are you wearing those silly socks?" and I said, "These are my house socks!!" in a very posh voice. I was very happy to overtake her near the end.'

The race was also an incentive for Will to quit smoking, a habit he has had trouble kicking for the past year.

'I was on 20 or 30 a day and I came back from Mexico and thought, "this is it, I can't do it any more". I went to see a hypnotist who helped me to stop for three months, but then I had a stressful week and went back on the fags. I went straight back to 20 a day. I ruined myself, my skin was really bad and I wasn't sleeping very well. Again I went to see my hypnotist and now I've stopped again. She gets it into your subconscious how bad it is to smoke. She told me what it does to my voice and said if you are a serious singer you wouldn't smoke, so I say that as a mantra to myself.'

Apart from the odd, ahem, drink, Will has very few vices, even kicking caffeine out of his diet for four months during the tour. He tries to drink

A sense of humar loss

Happy Chappy

a lot of water and eat a fair amount of fruit. He admits that staying in shape has a lot to do with his job.

'I do try and think about appearance – vanity is definitely a motivation in this business. There are so many diets out there where you give up things but I don't think they are good for you. I don't like the idea of giving up one main food source. I try to think about what I'm eating but I don't let it rule my life – if I fancy a curry I'll have one. When you meet people in real life they tend to look a lot smaller than they do on TV. So the other side of the coin is that if you are remotely big you look huge.'

There are also parts of Will's body that he's not too keen on the camera focusing in on.

'I have spindly legs, they're like chicken legs and I have a wonky jaw. I could have had an operation when I was 18 but it would have meant cracking my jaw and I wouldn't have been able to talk for ages, which with the way that I babble on, would have been a nightmare. Actually I have a lot of things I don't like, but doesn't everyone?! I sweat very quickly when I'm nervous, I literally drip sweat which is really disgusting, you can have an operation to snip the glands but I always think it's just going to come out in other places.'

Looking very young and very nervous at first ever TOTP's

Hello and I'll be your rep for today

Still looking very young but now
very weird (at first TOTP's)

Oh my God........

Parking ticket

Rest assured, there are some bits of his body he's keen you examined and made reassuringly nice comments about.

'I really like my bum. And I have good ankles. My bottom is very pert and high, my mum has always been known as having a great ass so I think I must get it from her. I want more comments about my bottom from people, so if you see me in the street feel free to say something nice about it. I want to win Rear Of The Year, because I have a great arse!'

Another beautiful Italian lady

A stylish man

'I think I'm so fashionable – haha.' Will is laughing, having just seen a picture of himself in a magazine which was poking fun out of his hair band and the sandals he was photographed wearing.

'I don't really mind what people think. Right from a young age I've probably worn some pretty ghastly things, (ghastly is one of my favourite words by the way, along with gymkhana!). My wardrobe is like a gymkhana of colour! I have always mixed and matched and have always been a bit scruffy. I was forever being told off at school for not having my top button done up.'

Will doesn't plan his wardrobe for the week, carefully selecting items of clothing to match his mood. Nor does he pick one outfit and wear it all week until it has to be scraped off him.

'Sometimes I will wear an outfit and the next day take it out and think it's not right for that day. It has to feel right.'

Will feels that his image has gradually changed over the past year and we are now starting to see the real him coming through in the clothes that he wears.

'I think publicly I've always been seen as someone suited and booted, but my style has just become more "me". I do like the suits because in

MTV – gorgeous girl, great sofa!

Serious Will – p.s. another good sofa

a way they feel like my work clothes and I wouldn't wear them away from the cameras.'

Helping him to let loose the inner Will through his clothes is his stylist Charty Durrant, who has been with him since the beginning.

'Charty is one of the best people I have met over the last year and a half. She's an inspirational person and I've learnt a lot from her. She taught me how to slowly push the boundaries of what I'm wearing. The best example I can give is the pale blue suit that I was photographed in and made the newspapers as one of the top ten outfits of the year. At the time some of the people around me were saying,

"Ooh, I'm not sure about that suit", but I was confident it would look great. And rather than getting in a fight about it, I was just laid back and said, "Well let's just see how it looks" and it looked great.'

He's also not fazed by other people's reactions to what he wears.

'I love it when the magazines criticise my clothes. I think it's brilliant. I don't take it personally. Sometimes I do look terrible but if I feel comfortable in what I'm wearing who cares what someone else thinks? There have been a few things I've looked back on and thought, "God, you look dire".'

Emailing @ Italian BMG headquarters

Tucked away behind his sofa in Will's flat is an enormous scrapbook that he constantly updates with clothes and looks that he tears out of magazines that he likes.

'I'm really into fashion and I like having a say in what I wear. I'm a big fan of Armani and have been for a few years. I think Burberry has some great new stuff. I think they're very me, as they're English but a bit modernised.'

Will is lucky enough to get sent trainers (he currently has about 30 pairs of Puma trainers which arrived in the post one day) but he's always on the lookout for more hats to add to his ever-growing collection.

'When I go out people say, "Are you wearing a hat to try and disguise yourself?" but I've always worn them. I find them really comforting and wear them a lot when I'm recording. Also I have terrible hair and it hides my bedhead. I don't think I've worn them enough on TV so when I promote the new album you will definitely see me wearing more hats.'

Will's sense of style has now extended to home furnishing as he's putting the finishing touches to his new house.

'It's a big investment but it keeps me motivated. I know I have to earn some money to pay off the mortgage. Although, one thing I've learnt is that you don't earn as much money as people seem to think you do.

Shoot this man

The phrase is 'smart casual'

Pleease..... shoot this man

Some people say I have a God complex

Not convinced

Everyone says, "Oh now you're a multi-millionaire" but that couldn't be further from the truth.'

The best thing for Will is that his house means he finally has somewhere he can shut out the world and relax.

'I do feel there are not many places where I'm not on show. So this house is my little area of solitude and comfort. My own space. Whenever I have free time I'm looking for things for the house.'

However, Will won't be calling upon the services of a well-known TV designer to help with the look of his new pad.

'I love Laurence Llewelyn-Bowen and I'm a big fan of *Changing Rooms*, but he wouldn't be allowed near my place. I'd rather eat my own toes than let him loose on my house.'

The fame game

If Will was to read everything that was written about him in the newspapers and magazines he would find himself thinking he must be suffering from a split personality disorder. On the one hand, there are his supporters who always put in a good word and say kind things about him and what he is doing, and then there are his detractors and for them, he can do nothing right.

'I'm careful of saying that I don't read the media, as that sounds like I'm above it. I do read interviews that I've given. Colin Firth once said, "I don't read interviews that I have given, as I have in the past and have been disappointed with the way they've portrayed me. But then perhaps I don't know myself and that is the real me". I love that. It's a really nice modest way to see yourself. I probably read half the things I do. I'm not good if

Top of the Pops Italy

I read nasty things that have been written about me because I can't really deal with it that well. If I read, "Will can't sing for s**t" and then I go into the studio, then that will be in the back of my mind.' Of course there are many publications that have written the odd nasty thing about Will, but there's only one newspaper that really bothers Will: the *Daily Mail*.

'They can say what they like about me. In fact they did! They wrote things about me which were totally inaccurate and unnecessary. My father has always told me, "If people really screw you, never forget it" and an elephant never forgets. Generally I don't think I've had a pounding. I'm sure I'll be knocked at some point and when it comes I hope that I can deal with it.'

Harry Potter on the move!

Receiving criticism from the media is to be expected, and by and large comes with the territory. It's more difficult to accept when it's from people on the street. When they are being rude. To your face.

'I'd just arrived back at Heathrow from one of my trips to Italy and I walked past these three men in their early twenties who shouted "batty boy" at me. I turned round and went up to them and said, "I'm sorry, what did you say to me?" and they were like, "I called you a batty boy, because you are one". They fronted up and I thought, "Here we go, I'm going to have a fight". I said, "No, I'm not a batty boy, I'm gay. There's a difference. That's not a nice thing to say to someone. Do you have a problem with me being gay? If you have a problem say it to my face" –

Anyone would think I have a furniture fetish!

they completely backed down and looked at the ground. Then the guy goes, "Ooh can I have an autograph?" I said, "You must be joking" and walked off. Then they said it again, so I turned round and asked again if they had a problem. By this stage people were looking and I turned and walked away. I was livid and completely shaking. I don't get cross that often and it was the closest I'd come to having a fight with someone. That's one of the downsides of celebrity. Under normal circumstances, I may have ended up in a rather different situation, but as a celebrity you sometimes have to bite your tongue.'

Despite the constant media attention, Will has been determined to live as much of a normal life as possible.

Autographs on the make

'This year has been one moment of normality after the next. Sunday night I got really trashed and was running up and down the Fulham Road playing a game of chase with buses, and I think 'Well, why can't I do that?' I wouldn't have done that last year, I would have been too conscious of someone maybe taking a photograph. I've come to accept fame and realise that with it, you can do amazing things. The obvious things are charity work and setting the right example for people. One of the best things that happened was after coming out in the papers, this chap came up to me in a pub and he said, "I saw you had come out in the papers and now I've just come out to my family, thanks for being so honest". I thought that was amazing because if I could help one person then it's been worth it.'

He's also come to accept that the media focusing on his life is just another part of the job.

'I find the media fascinating. They say it's a sign of a healthy capitalist society when people have their health, employment and a house to live in and then they look at the supposed higher echelons of society to aspire to. I try not to set myself up to be a perfect person because I'm not one. I like the fact that I'm pictured in magazines looking normal, doing normal things. Personally I love seeing David Beckham looking absolutely gorgeous but another part of me would really like to see him looking minging first thing in the morning. So we all think the same things. We all have that voyeuristic side to us which is why I can't be annoyed if someone takes a picture of me.'

A very short chapter about relationships

'They're non-existent and I'm single.' Being famous has its downsides – and one of them is that it is much harder to find that perfect someone.

'I'm 24 and have never had a serious relationship, so I'm trying to be a bit more proactive about it, although I'm not really sure how to do that. I joke with friends that coming out in the papers was like an advert to 65 million people and yet I still can't find someone! It does make me laugh. A lot of my friends have been going out with someone for a while, and I don't usually feel lonely, but occasionally I do. Particularly in hotel rooms abroad. It's nice being in great hotels but you look at the romantic, opulent room and the massive bed and think, "I'm in bed on my own with a cup of cocoa".'

Will isn't even concerned that he might meet someone and they would run off and sell their stories to the papers.

'I trust my judgement and think I'm a really good judge of character. I believe I would know if they were trying to be with me just because I am

famous. I don't really get that many offers to be honest, which isn't good for the old ego. If someone was an arsehole and we split up and they went to the papers I would just be disappointed. But what more can you say? I don't want to be paranoid and always be thinking, "Oh why are you with me?".'

But it doesn't get Will down and he remains optimistic that someone will come along soon.

'I'm quite romantic and don't really meet that many people that I really like. I think people think I'm playing the field but I'm really not. I'm very much ready for a relationship now and I'm keeping my eyes open, but it will be a momentous day when it happens.'

Will Live!

Some had camped overnight. By 8.30 in the morning there was a queue winding its way from the entrance gate off into the distance. Fans had come from as far as California and South Africa. No, this isn't a description of the first week of Wimbledon, it was the sight that greeted early morning risers one Friday in July at Killerton House on the outskirts of Exeter. The site for Will Live!

It seemed fitting that Will chose his first solo concert to be in his university town where he had spent three years learning the lessons that have turned him into the entertainer he is today.

A sunny evening @ Killerton House — HOORAY!

A colourful audience

My new Yoga position

'It's very much like a second home to me. The Cathedral Green was always one of my favourite places. It was quite funny as when friends were looking for me everyone would say they could find me on the green. I am still in love with Exeter – it's got so much character and, of course, so many great memories for me.'

The idea for the outside music event started in the summer of 2002 when Will had a meeting with Liz Hogan at Postive Action South West, a charity Will had already become involved with while at university.

'We had a meeting at the end of the summer and I said the things that I could bring to the charity were profile, cash and helping to raise awareness

for Aids and HIV in the South West. We all agreed that a concert would be the best way to do this and Liz suggested the Exeter Festival. So we ran with it, primarily as something for Positive Action. But as it turned out it was perfect timing for me. I hadn't been around for six months, I would be able to play some of my new tracks and it would be the first gig on my own.'

Unlike some concerts where bands turn up five minutes before going on stage, do their bit and then leave in a cloud of dust, Will and his team were involved in every element of the concert, from ticketing, the production on the night, the running order of the gig, to the way the stage was decorated and even the music that was played over the loudspeakers before showtime.

A tempting Italian snack?

'I compiled a warm-up CD of all my favourite songs. That was fun because depending on what songs I chose, I could decide on the mood of the event. I had Grace Jones, Joan Armatrading, Nina Simone and Bill Withers on there, nothing upbeat, just some nice songs to give a chilled-out vibe. We did so much of the organisation and we tried to cut so many corners, cost-wise, to try and save money. The Indian backdrop and the rugs on the floor of the stage were all simple. To be fair my assistant Faye was doing most of the organising, along with Exeter council, as I was in the studio.'

The support on the night came from a samba band called Street Heat and Brighton's Sarah Bennett, a Macy Gray lookalike singer/songwriter

Richard and I pretend to work (whilst drinking heavily!)

with an amazing voice who took to the stage with just an acoustic guitar. Again Will was involved in choosing his support acts.

'One of my management team spotted Sarah performing at a Prince's Trust concert. It only took one listen to one of her songs to realise she had to play. She's so cool.'

Backstage Will's pre-gig nerves were calmed when he received a letter and a special pin from the Mayor declaring him to be an Ambassador of Exeter – 'I was thinking that they really didn't want me as an ambassador particularly if they had seen me drunk in the student union' – and so blessed with a perfect summer's evening and now with the

Don't **** with this 'cool' dude!

backing of Exeter's governing officials, Will's band took to the stage just before 9pm to an expectant 6,000 strong crowd.

'The way the show started I wanted Chris, the drummer, to walk on and start playing, then Thomas the percussionist do the same, then Howard the pianist, then John the bassist and then Joseph the guitarist. Then I started singing off stage, which as you know is my neat little trick and always seems to work. I felt the show was really fluid by doing that.'

The two-and-a-half-hour-show was split into two sets, the first including the songs: 'Ticket To Love', 'Cruel To Be Kind', 'Lovestruck', 'Dance The Night Away', 'Alibi Of Love', 'Roxanne' and 'Over You'. After a short

THE BAND!

interval Will returned to perform four acoustic numbers – 'You And I', 'Fields Of Gold', 'Anything Is Possible', 'Light My Fire' – before all the band rejoined him for 'Time Enough', 'Lover Won't You Stay', 'Superstitious', 'Evergreen' and a fully fleshed out second outing of 'You And I'.

'I don't think I've ever played in front of a crowd who were so up for it. It really lived up to my expectations. I wanted it to be that type of atmosphere, very relaxed, very joyous and a real laugh. There wasn't anything over the top, I didn't come out to fireworks and a big build-up. The old stuff went down well and I felt had been moved on musically, there was no programming, and the band made the old songs really

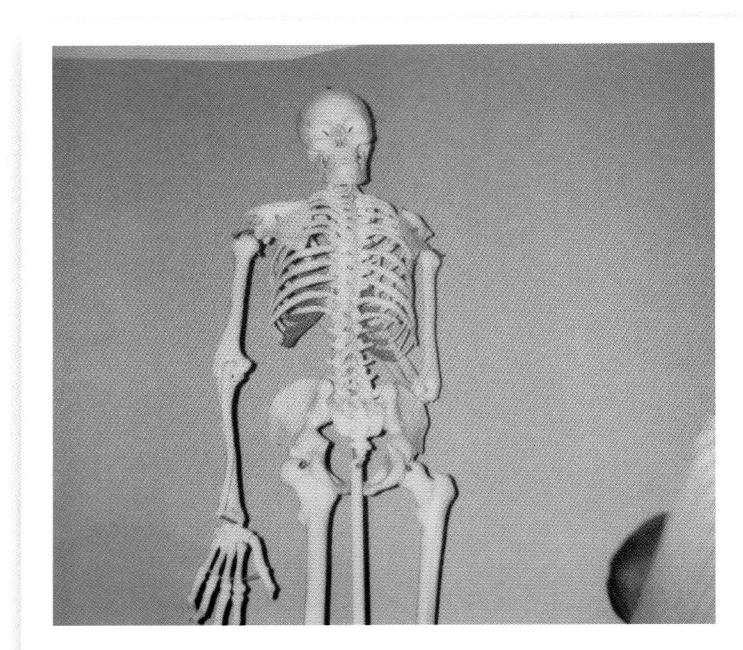

Sometimes I work myself into the grand

come to life and in a way, sound so different. The new material seemed to go down well; 'Alibi Of Love' is a beautiful song, but difficult to sing and I'm not sure I nailed that one fully. I came off after the first set and I thought, "I knew I wouldn't be 100 per cent happy and I know I would be more insecure about the new stuff because I wanted it to be perfect". One of the other new songs I did, 'Time Enough', went down really well even though I forgot my words, I realised that no one would know as they'd never heard it before – haha."

But it was the acoustic set, with Will sitting on stage on a stool wearing a green panama hat accompanied only by Joseph on guitar, that will live long in the memory for Mr Young.

Patchwork Man

'I could have pissed myself I was so happy! It's what I love doing the most – sitting down with a guitar and just singing. The sun had just gone down and it made the whole festival a lot more intimate.'

He was pleased the covers he'd chosen received such a warm reception too.

'I was a bit worried about doing three covers, I thought two was enough in any show, particularly with my history of being the "karaoke king" of covers. 'Roxanne' was such a hit, 'Fields Of Gold' is part of my set and has been for the last year and I thought I had to do a Stevie Wonder track so I chose 'Superstitious'. It was tough to rehearse but it went really well. Of course I didn't tell anyone that I taped the words to 'Roxanne' to the stage.'

The crowd numbers were swollen by Will's friends and family who all made the trip down to Exeter to lend him their support.

'I was so chuffed they all came down. Most of my close friends came. They mean so much to me and it made a huge difference to have them there. The funniest thing was looking out into the crowd and seeing my friends Andy and Sarah. I could see this little five-year-old on her dad's shoulders and then next to them was this 23-year-old woman on top of a man who was buckling under the strain. It was so funny to see his face between her legs. He gave me this look of sheer pain as she was bouncing around. I gave her a little wave and she got more excited and poor Andy almost died!'

Photoshoot in Germany

As the happy throng headed for the exits with a rousing rendition of 'You And I' reverberating in their ears, there was only one thing left for Will to do. An important post-gig ritual that couldn't be ignored. The only thing that could assist his concert come-down. An essential requirement of any musician's routine.

'And then we went and had some beers. Many beers.'

Mafia

CLEAR

Will and William (the puppy!)